LORD, help me to *Flourish*

A COLORING DEVOTIONAL

NATHALIE VILLENEUVE & LEILA GRANDEMANGE

Lord, Help Me to Flourish • A Coloring Devotional
copyright © 2016 Nathalie Villeneuve and Leila Grandemange

first printing: November, 2016
ISBN: 978-0-9975658-1-2

Printed in the United States of America

Sunny Ville
PUBLISHING
www.sunnyvillepublishing.com

Table of Contents

About the Coloring Devotional

FLOURISH is such a beautiful word! It brings to mind images of picturesque fields covered with all sorts of colorful flowers thriving under the warm summer sun. "Flourish" is also a very meaningful word because it captures God's desire for each one of us—to thrive, prosper, and bloom in every area of our life! Is that something that speaks to you? If so, this book was designed just for you by co-authors Nathalie Villeneuve and Leila Grandemange. Their vision:

To help women flourish in faith while experiencing God through the Creative Arts.

In 2016, Nathalie and Leila prayerfully embarked on a journey to create a unique book that would combine a relaxing and creative activity like coloring with the study of God's Word. Hence the idea came about of a "Coloring Devotional!" In this book you'll find Nathalie's inspirational paintings and coloring pages, along with Leila's heartwarming devotionals and the study questions beautifully woven together into one message! Each theme was prayerfully chosen to help you experience God in a more personal way while discovering what it means to flourish for His purposes and glory!

Lord, Help Me To Flourish is not only the title of this book, it's also the authors' earnest prayer, because flourishing is only possible with help from above. So let's begin with a simple prayer:

> DEAR LORD,
>
> Help me to flourish. I give you my hopes and dreams, my past, present and future, and all that I hold dear. Please open my eyes to the potential you place within me and help me to break through my outer shell—all the fear, shame, sin, and anything that is keeping me from the life you intended for me. Please also give me the courage to reach out and invite others along this magnificent faith-filled flourishing journey. I entrust my life, my family, and my friends into Your loving Hands.
>
> In Jesus' name, Amen.

Those who are planted in the house of the Lord shall flourish in the courts of our God.

—Psalm 92:13 NKJV

How to Use This Book

We are so excited that you've chosen this coloring devotional to be a part of your quiet time with the Lord, or to work through with your small group (see guidelines on page 98). Each coloring devotional has six pages and is divided into three sections to give you a unique creative arts experience while you flourish in your faith. We invite you to flow through each section prayerfully and expectantly, and to anticipate a vibrant encounter with God as you observe the paintings, read the devotionals, journal, and color. Take all the time you need—Rest, Relax, Enjoy!

Observe the Paintings—Nathalie Villenueve describes her experience while painting in the "About the Painting" section, and then invites you to prayerfully soak in the colors, textures, movement, and emotion in her paintings. Let the painting speak. What thoughts and emotions come to mind?

Read the Devotionals—Leila Grandemange shares her heart in the devotionals and invites you to reflect more on each topic with the questions that follow. Each devotional was written with the painting in mind. Pray, linger in God's Word, and allow the Holy Spirit to speak to your heart through the painting and text. If you're working through this book with a group, this is a great time to connect with others and discuss the questions.

Color and Journal Your Flourishing Thoughts—Gather your coloring pencils and take all the time you need to color while meditating on the topic. The experience will be calming, freeing, and even revelatory when you connect with the image and tune in to that still small voice. What do you hear? Journal your flourishing thoughts on the lines provided—write a prayer, jot down your favorite Bible verse, or just doodle and dream. This is your space to connect with God and flourish in your faith!

May this coloring devotional be a place where you can freely share your thoughts and emotions, and find oneness with God through art.

Life lessons from the nursery: Broken crayons can still color.
— Unknown

Flourishing Faith

— About the Painting —

As I was painting "Faith" late into the evening while listening to soaking music there were no hesitations in my brush strokes! A voice inside me was telling me to not force anything and to let the Holy Spirit guide me. I loved seeing how the colors were transitioning from light to dark under the soft and fluid movements of my hand. As I dipped my brush in the thick gold paint, my eye glanced at the silhouette and I knew what color I would be mixing next. I scooped up an equal amount of blue, red, and brown to create one of my favorite colors . . . dark eggplant. I chose this color to fully contrast with the lighter gold and vanilla tones in my artwork. My hand moved with the same ease and flowing assurance from beginning to end! This painting is the perfect example of what we can accomplish through Faith.

— Pause and Reflect —

What thoughts come to mind as you observed the colors, textures, movement, and emotion in the painting?

Flourishing Faith

What does Flourishing Faith look like? Imagine a beautiful lady, like the one we are about to color, basking in the warm glow of God's presence. She's kneeling before her Creator with out-stretched arm humbly acknowledging that she's far from perfect, and that her ability to flourish is only possible as she remains in Him. "Lord, help me to flourish," is her prayer as she offers God her life and everything she holds dear—her family, work, and all her hopes and dreams. She lingers in the

light of God's presence and her countenance radiates peace and joy. Each morning she comes before her Lord to share her heart and listen. . . soon beautiful blossoms emerge and she becomes even more beautiful, patient, loving, and kind. Her focus is not on herself, rather it's turned outward to love her neighbor, and her heart is fully devoted to her beloved Savior Jesus Christ.

I know what you're thinking however: Does this person really exist? I'd sure love to look like her! I can relate. For years I was like a seed, lying stagnant within the ground as if trapped within a shell. "Lord, help me to flourish," was not my prayer. It was more like, "Lord, please help me to survive!" I suppose I mostly went to God when I needed something, but I was not really connected to Him through a personal relationship. After years of trying to thrive on my own, and struggling with worry,

anxiety, and fear, I finally looked up and prayed, "Lord, please help me to flourish. I desperately want to break free from this shell and discover the joy of living in the light. Please help me to find my purpose!"

Thankfully, God heard my cry for help—"For everyone that calls on the name of the Lord shall be saved!" (Romans 10:13). He explained that my journey would begin with an uprooting. That meant leaving behind all the dirt that clung to my roots. He would then plant me within His garden, a place filled with everything I'd need to flourish—His very Words and the light of His constant presence would cause a never-ending cycle of blooms! He also explained that the process from seedling to blooms may have its painful moments—there would be times of pruning, shaping, and even cut-ting off the dead branches if needed. Though I felt a twinge of fear, one look in His loving eyes was enough to know that I could trust Him. So I offered Him my life (my tiny seed of faith), and before I knew it tiny sprouts broke through the earth and flourished into beautiful blooms! God affec-tionately named each one—love, joy, peace, patience, kindness—while letting me know that many more blooms would eventually come, revealing even more of His lovely attributes. His Word, prayer, praise, and fellowship are now the nutrients that feed my soul, and my hope is firmly planted in Christ who is faithful to complete the work He began in me. I am a work in progress—Hallelujah!!

Dear friend, it's really no coincidence that this image of the girl kneeling before God with out-stretched arm asking, "Lord, help me to flourish," was also chosen for the front cover. It sets the

Flourishing Faith

tone for every other topic in this book, because it is only by coming before Him daily, by faith, that we can thrive, prosper, and bloom in any area of our lives. Flourishing Faith is therefore a life-long journey of establishing our roots deep into God's Word, and seeking the warmth of His love. Think of the tiny seedling that grows its roots, which then breaks through its outer shell and becomes the sprout seeking the life-given nutrients of the sun, which then produces the stems, buds, and the myriad of blooms. There is constant movement towards the destiny for which the seed was created. Your faith was created to flourish, dear friend. Just plant your roots deep into the fertile soil of God and get ready for one of the most miraculous, challenging, yet fulfilling journeys you'll ever experience!

Maybe you are that tiny seed desperately wanting to emerge from your shell, or maybe you're in the process of being uprooted and replanted. Some of you are already full of colorful blooms and want to share your joy with others. Wherever you are on your faith journey, I'd like to encourage you to travel with one hand stretched forward towards your goal, and one hand reaching back to help others along the way. We all need each other to realize God's plan and to flourish in every area of our lives—family, faith, friendships, work and play—and girlfriends are some of the best companions to brighten our path! Oh Lord, help us to flourish, for Your purpose and glory! Amen.

1.   After reading the devotional text, how would you define Flourishing Faith?

_____

_____

_____

2.   Write Hebrews 11:1 from your Bible, then hide it in your heart.

_____

_____

3.   Where do you find yourself on the journey of faith?

_____

_____

_____

_____

_____

It's time to color and journal your flourishing thoughts!

Flourishing Faith

*For everyone that calls on the name of
the Lord shall be saved!*

—Romans 10:13

Journal your flourishing thoughts about Faith.

And above all,
take up the shield
of faith . . .

Ephesians 6:16

Lord, help me to flourish in Faith!

Flourishing Friendship

— About the Painting —

Will you lean on me, dear friend?

I will point you towards God's love.

I will offer gentleness, generosity,

understanding, and support.

I will always encourage you to hold on
to your hopes and dreams.

I offer you my friendship as an everlasting bloom.

A source of comfort and joy!

Love,

Your friend

— Pause and Reflect —

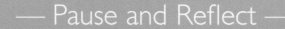

*What thoughts come to mind as you observed
the colors, textures, movement, and emotion in the painting?*

Flourishing Friendship

Friendship is one of God's most precious gifts and the source of incredible joy, yet this gift can also cause tremendous heartache if not handled correctly. Friendship, simply defined, is a relationship between two individuals who have a mutual affection for each other. True friendship is "life-enhancing" and is often revealed by such qualities as mutual trust, respect, commitment, loyalty, and love. Isn't that

what we all long for in a friend? Yet if we're honest, we recognize that we all fall short in one or more of these areas. That said, I truly believe that friendship can only be understood and achieved with help from above. Let's reflect on the meaning of friendship and ask the Lord for guidance on this all important, possibly life-changing topic.

Close your eyes for a moment and think of a close friend. Who came to your mind? I'd like to share who came to my mind: my friend and the co-author of this book, Nathalie Villeneuve. Our collaboration on this project is a beautiful example of what happens when women come together in faith and friendship, inspiring each other towards their God-given dreams. This book you are holding is the fruit of that friendship, and we are both incredibly humbled and grateful for this journey! In fact, this painting of the two women arm in arm could be us, leaning on each other for support throughout this venture. Life can be so rough, and we need each other's encouraging words more than we know. Notice how the petals are falling, as if symbolizing tears or broken dreams. I sensed God saying that some of you reading this devotional have been deeply wounded in friendships and that your dreams have fallen to the wayside. Now look at where her friend is pointing . . . she's reaching up and out as if encouraging her to hope in God. Dear friend, please don't allow past broken relationships to define your future. The enemy would like you to give up on people and to do life on your own. But God created friendship for a reason. Read these encouraging words from Ecclesiastes 4:9-12:

> Two people are better off than one, for they can help each other succeed. If one person falls, the other can reach out and help. But someone who falls alone is in real trouble . . . A person standing alone can be attacked and defeated, but two can stand back-to-back and conquer.

God knows friends have great power to influence us for good or evil. Choosing friends is like choosing teammates for a sport. So let's imagine what a winning team might look like. When choosing a close friend ask, "Are we like-minded, having the same goal, to become more like Christ? If the answer is "yes," then there's a good chance you just found an amazing teammate! Now this doesn't mean that we exclude everyone else. But we must be careful. The writer of 1 Corinthians 15 warns us that bad company corrupts good character. Proverbs 13:20 also tells us that if we walk with the wise, we become wise. But if we associate with fools, we get into trouble. Most coaches will agree that choosing teammates who have the same goal and are like-minded is vital if you want to win, and attitude will play a large part. I used to love watching my daughter's volleyball games. Whether the players hit the ball in or out,

Flourishing Friendship

their teammates cheered them on. They'd clap, give a "high 5," or console each other with a hug when needed. They always had a positive attitude! Good friends encourage you to achieve your dreams, they rejoice when you succeed, comfort you when you fail, pick you up when you're down, and remain faithful through thick and thin. Proverbs 17:17 tells us that "A friend is always loyal, and a brother is born to help in time of need."

One of the hardest things for friends, however, is to confront each other when needed. The New Testament affirms that a true friend is one who speaks the truth in love (Ephesians 4:15-16). And if we're the recipient of a correction, it is our role to prayerfully listen with humility and a teachable spirit. Just the other day a friend gently pointed out some negative self-talk that slipped out of my mouth, and she continued by encouraging me to believe in myself. I'm so thankful for such friends who unashamedly pull me towards God's love and help me fulfill my God-given destiny—to become more like Christ. I'd also like to be a friend who fits that description. Will you pray with me for guidance?

Dear Heavenly Father, There's so much I don't understand about friendship. Please protect me and help me to choose friends that would draw me towards You. Help me to be the kind of friend that reflects your love. Fill my heart with compassion, mercy, and grace, and help me to forgive others, just as You've forgiven me. Give me eyes to see the best in my friends, and when they're down, help me to lift them up and point them to You, the most faithful friend the world could ever know!
In Jesus' name, Amen.

1. After reading the devotional text, how would you define Flourishing Friendship?

_____

_____

_____

2. Write down Proverbs 17:17 from your Bible, then hide it in your heart.

_____

_____

_____

3. How could you be a better friend?

_____

_____

_____

_____

_____

It's time to color and journal your flourishing thoughts!

Flourishing Friendship

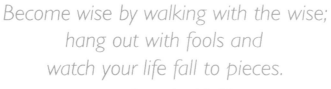

Become wise by walking with the wise;
hang out with fools and
watch your life fall to pieces.
—*Proverbs 13:20 The Message*

Journal your flourishing thoughts about Friendship.

Friends are
flowers that
never fade.
—Anonymous

Lord, help me to flourish in Friendship!

Flourishing Creativity

As I made my way up the stairs leading to the stage at church, I was a little nervous to be painting in front of an audience. I prayed for God to keep my inspiration flowing and be led by the music, dancers, and Holy Spirit.

While painting, I felt an awakening of all my senses. I became very calm and focused on my blank canvas, I wasn't intimidated anymore. I feel like the whole experience and the painting itself were a gift from God . . . His way of telling me, "You got this, girl." This painting represents the "free creative spirit" within us. God created us in His image; therefore we can create and be a blessing to those around us!

— Pause and Reflect —

What thoughts come to mind as you observed
the colors, textures, movement, and emotion in the painting?

Flourishing Creativity

While living in France studying to get my teaching degree in ballet, I was very fortunate to participate in a class for young children called *Creative Movement*. Each week the nearby school would bring in a class of preschoolers and our "job" was to awaken their creativity. We were specifically told to avoid demonstrating or giving solutions but rather to use imagery and simple cues as guidelines for each exercise.

One exercise involved handing out colorful flow-y scarves and asking each child to find a way to get the scarf from one side of the room to the next. Sounds easy enough, right? The catch was, they weren't allowed to use arms, hands, or legs. The only imagery given was that a breeze was blowing and the sun was shining. Our goal was to teach them to run with grace while lifting their upper bodies. We didn't tell them this of course. There was a moment of silent reflection, the pianist started playing, and then the magic . . . I watched in awe. One child draped the scarf across his chest and took off running. The scarf held in place by the sheer fact that he ran with head, chest, arms, and eyes lifted. Guess what just happened? Not only did he learn how to run with presence and poise, he was also being creative by using his own imagination to solve a problem. It was truly inspiring watching the children express themselves and seeing their sweet spirits bubble with joy! We were not only teaching them to dance, we also fostered an environment for creativity and confidence to flourish!

Have you ever wanted to be "creative" but didn't really know how? Or maybe you felt you lacked the confidence or skills? I'm sure we've all struggled with those feelings. Some of you may even be thinking, "Well, I'm just not the creative type." I'd like to dispel a few myths. EVERYONE was born with the potential to create, because we were created in the image of God. The very first act recorded in scripture (Genesis 1:3) reveals God's explosive creative energy unleashed into the darkness— "And God said, 'Let there be light!'" And God's creative power continued to express itself through the creation of the sun, moon, and stars, all the animals, the infinite varieties of plants, and of course His greatest masterpiece, mankind! As image bearers of a creative God, we have the potential for creativity literally written into our DNA—like Father, like son! Think about the young child, like those in my dance class, or even your own children who freely color, play make-believe, and create all sorts of interesting things without fear what others may think. Studies have shown that we are born creative but that as we grow up we unlearn how to be creative. The good news is, our creative core can be awakened at any time regardless of our age, ability, or profession. So what exactly is "creativity" and how do we tap into it?

Flourishing Creativity

Creativity is simply the act of turning our innovative ideas into reality. It involves two steps: thinking and producing. So if you have ideas but don't act on them, you are imaginative but not creative. This is where it takes faith, to step out into the unknown and trust God to turn our imaginative ideas into reality! The story Nathalie tells while painting at church is a perfect illustration. As I look closer at the image she painted, I notice a key. What do you think that key represents? Do you notice her looking up, as if looking to God for inspiration? The key she's holding represents her connection and trust in God as He creates in her and through her for His purpose and glory. So whether I'm writing, dancing, painting, cooking, raising my children, or facing a problem at work, creativity flourishes as I place my trust in Christ. Jesus says in John 15:5, "Yes, I am the vine; you are the branches. Those who remain in Me, and I in them, will bear much fruit. For apart from Me you can do nothing."

So grab that scarf, my friend, and find a way to get it from where you are now to where you want to be. The music is playing, the breeze is blowing, and the sun is shining. Are you ready to run and awaken your creative core? Invite God into all your activities, find opportunities to nurture your talents, and trust God to make your dreams come true! The sky's the limit to be creative, and each coloring page is a perfect opportunity to spread your creative wings and soar!

1.   After reading the devotional text, how would you define Flourishing Creativity?

_____

_____

_____

2.   Copy John 15:5 from your Bible, then hide it in your heart.

_____

_____

3.   Do you see yourself as creative? Write down one goal that you feel will help you awaken your creative core.

_____

_____

_____

_____

_____

_____

It's time to color and journal your flourishing thoughts!

Flourishing Creativity

*I am the vine, and you are the branches. If you abide in Me
and I in you, you will bear great fruit. Without Me,
you will accomplish nothing.*
—John 15:5, The Voice

Journal your flourishing thoughts about Creativity.

We have
the mind
of Christ.
I Corinthians 2:16

Lord, help me to flourish in Creativity!

Flourishing Hope

— About the Painting —

She dances on the beach

with her arms lifted high towards the sky.

A cool breeze filters through her fingers

and she feels free!

As she twirls around and around,

sand gets into her shoes.

She stops for a brief instant,

smiles and continues to dance

as hope fills her dancing heart.

— Pause and Reflect —

What thoughts come to mind as you observed
the colors, textures, movement, and emotion in the painting?

Flourishing Hope

Have you ever had that sweet "knowing" that all things were going to work out for good? HOPE is a confident expectation of GOOD things from God. It's truly a beautiful thing to have, but when it's lacking, the heart feels heavy. Have you ever tried to dance with a heavy heart? It's not fun, I've been there.

Most of my life was spent trying to dance to a tune I didn't care for and barely understood. One minute I was twirling to a delightful waltz, and the next minute the music changed to a roaring rock while my insides were screaming, "TIME OUT!" Occasionally the music would slow down and come to a halt. I'd catch my breath, wipe off the sweat (it was usually tears at this point), and melt to the floor. Nothing seemed to make sense, not the choice of music, nor the rhythm, and certainly not the choreography. I was hoping for more of a *Cinderella* story with a happy ending. Often I'd find my-

Leila painting "Hope."

self heavy-hearted and pleading with Heaven asking, "Who's the maestro? What on earth are you doing!" Exhaustion and bouts of depression eventually took hold of me and I began to wonder, "What if this is not the life I was meant for?" I desperately needed some hope . . .

When I was in a season of discouragement, my artist friend (Nathalie) invited me to her painting workshop. I really had no time. But then I saw the image of the beautiful ballerina we would paint—a free spirit flowing with the breeze, sunshine and sand, calm ocean waters, a peaceful beach setting . . . even the birds appeared to join in her dance! She embodied everything I longed for. Her very essence drew me to paint and with each stroke of the brush my heart fluttered with joy.

Proud of my new work of art, I carried it home and placed it by a window. Each day I look at it I smile and sense the hope that she radiates from her being. I admit that I'd love it if each day of my life resembled that of the dancer on the beach. Goodness, who doesn't prefer sunshine and sandy beaches! But as I reflected more on the painting, and my longing for hope, I was reminded that "hope," the kind God gives, is not dependent on my circumstances. It's dependent on the knowledge that God is good, that He loves me, and that He is working ALL things together for my good (Romans 8:28). I began to understand that my longing for peaceful water, warm sunshine, and gentle winds is really a longing for Christ. Only in Him can those things be found. What I discovered is that hope is not a feeling, it's a person, and that person is Jesus Christ! He radiates everything I long for—love, joy, peace, patience, kindness, and everything good, lovely, and pure. His very essence draws me to Himself, and in His presence is fullness of joy. Each day that I look to HIM, my heart is filled with hope!

Flourishing Hope

While the music around me still seems chaotic at times, my ears are now tuned in to a different song, each note from Heaven calms my spirit and helps me to trust in God's wisdom and plan. The definition of hope has taken on new meaning for me. Hope is not only the confident expectation of GOOD things from God. It is also my ability to give up the desire to define "good things," and to TRUST in God. Hope and trust are like two sisters walking hand in hand. We cannot have one without the other.

How about you, dear friend, are you in need of hope? Do you really believe that God cares about your situation? I'm sure we've all struggled with believing God at times. Sometimes I think we just need a friend to look us in the eyes and say, "Don't give up!" "Believe in yourself!" or "This too shall pass." Hope is like wings, but not just any wings—strong, powerful wings that raise us up when the storms of life weigh us down. " . . . but those who HOPE in the Lord will renew their strength. They will soar on wings like eagles; they will run and not grow weary, they will walk and not be faint" (Isaiah 40:31).

As you color the ballerina on the beach, imagine yourself letting go of all your worries, fears, and anything that's weighing you down. Release them into the wind and trust that God will care for all your needs. It's your time to dance, dear friend!

May the God of hope fill you with all joy and peace as you trust in him.

—Romans 15:13

1. After reading the devotional text, how would you define Flourishing Hope?

_____

_____

_____

2. Write down Jeremiah 29:11 from your Bible, then hide it in your heart.

_____

_____

3. What does it mean to have a "living hope"? Read 1 Peter 1:3 then share your thoughts.

_____

_____

_____

_____

_____

It's time to color and journal your flourishing thoughts!

Flourishing Hope

*Rejoice in hope, be patient in tribulation,
be constant in prayer.*
—Romans 12:2

Journal your flourishing thoughts about Hope.

_____
_____
_____
_____
_____
_____
_____
_____
_____
_____
_____
_____

This hope we have
as an anchor
of the soul
Hebrews 6:19

Lord, help me to flourish in Hope!

Flourishing Words

— About the Painting —

As she is stepping out of the ashes, her beauty arises.

Her heart longs to express her gratitude

and she wants to shout her thanks for God's grace.

As she raises her hand to praise Him,

she touches her mouth, giving herself permission to speak.

A river of kind words rushing out like gentle waves,

clear, light, pure, and refreshing.

Clothed in white, she wanders towards her new life.

She is still feeling undeserving but she rejoices

that He made her His bride.

She will stand firm in her faith and now trusts

that God will guide her every step.

She will forever speak of her love for Him,

"Your praise, Lord, will always be on my lips!"

— Pause and Reflect —

What thoughts come to mind as you observed
the colors, textures, movement, and emotion in the painting?

Flourishing Words

I love roses! I love them so much that in our last home we planted roses of almost every color. Roses are popular perennial plants that come in a variety of colors. But their stems are often armed with sharp thorns or spines. If I could compare words to a plant, it would be a rose-bush . . .

Often while strolling through my rose garden, I'd lean over to take in their sweet aroma. The fragrance

would calm and lift my spirits, much like kind words to the soul. While tending to my roses, I've also been pricked. If you've ever been injured by a thorn, you'll relate to the sharp, sudden, unexpected sting and the lingering pain that ensues! Like the rose-bush, every word has the potential to fill our world with beauty or to pierce our heart. I'm reminded of my young school days . . . the reckless words spoken by some of my peers caused wounds that took years to recover from. I'm sure we've all been on either the giving or receiving end of hurtful words at some point. Many of us even speak hurtful words over our own lives with negative self talk—"I'm not smart enough," "I'm not pretty enough," "I'm ugly, fat, stupid . . ." I can imagine God wincing in pain, as if pricked by a thorn, over each harmful word spoken about His children. Proverbs 18:21 says that DEATH and LIFE are in the power of the tongue, and James 3 tells us that people can tame all kinds of animals, but no one can tame the tongue. Winston Churchill echoed this thought by saying, "We are masters of the unsaid words, but slaves of those we let slip out."

Thankfully, once we receive Jesus as our Savior, and make Him Lord of our lives, everything becomes new! Imagine trading your old heart with all its broken pieces, hurts, and painful memories, for a brand new heart filled God's love! Matthew 12:34 says that "out of the abundance of the heart the mouth speaks." A heart full of love speaks love. A heart full of peace speaks peace. A heart full of hope sheds healing, encouragement, and inspiration everywhere it goes. We may even prefer silence on occasion while we listen and learn from others. As we submit our wills to God on a daily basis, our thoughts, words, and even our actions come under the guidance of the Holy Spirit. Not only does our "talk" become pleasing to God, but we also begin to "walk our talk" and become authentic from the inside out. Flourishing words are therefore words that are birthed from a new heart that is submitted to God and filled with His love. These words are infused with LIFE and build up those who hear them. I recall hearing such words from my loved ones over the years. Thanks to their kind words, I've experienced comfort, encouragement, and healing, and gone on to achieve numerous dreams! I'd like to imagine that each time words of blessing are spoken, beautiful roses flourish in Heaven. But not just any roses. These are void of thorns! Can you picture the joy and freedom of walking, running, and even playing in a garden filled with thorn-free rose bushes? I can imagine that the woman in the Flourishing Words painting is walking through such a garden. Notice the ashes and the rose petals falling behind her. It's as if she's stepping away from her past into a new way of thinking, feeling, and speaking. I also love

Flourishing Words

how she's touching her lips, as if dedicating her words to her beloved Savior. May God's Kingdom come to earth and may His precious life- giving words grace the gardens of our life!

Dear friend, if words truly hold the power of life and death, and if no one can tame the tongue except God, wouldn't it be fitting to start our day with prayer? The following prayer is inspired from Psalm 19:4, Psalm 141:3, and Ephesians 4:29. Will you pray with me?

Dear Heavenly Father, I touch my lips as a symbolic gesture and ask you to infuse my words, whether spoken or written, with LIFE and the sweet aroma of Your love. May the words of my mouth and the meditations of my heart be pleasing to You. Please set a guard over my mouth and keep watch over the door of my lips, that no unwholesome talk would come out, but only that which is helpful to build others up. Thank you for helping me to step away from the ashes of my old life and into a new way of speaking. O Lord, my Rock and my Redeemer. Amen.

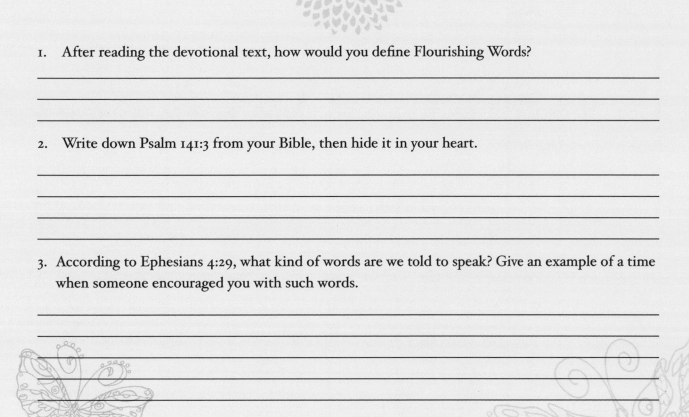

1. After reading the devotional text, how would you define Flourishing Words?

_____

_____

_____

2. Write down Psalm 141:3 from your Bible, then hide it in your heart.

_____

_____

_____

_____

3. According to Ephesians 4:29, what kind of words are we told to speak? Give an example of a time when someone encouraged you with such words.

_____

_____

_____

_____

_____

It's time to color and journal your flourishing thoughts!

Flourishing Words

*May the words of my mouth
and the meditation of my heart
be pleasing to you, O Lord,
my rock and my redeemer.*
—Psalm 19:14

Journal your flourishing thoughts about Words.

_____

_____

_____

_____

_____

_____

_____

_____

_____

_____

_____

_____

_____

_____

*Kind words are like
honey—sweet to
the soul and healthy
for the body.*
—Proverbs 16:24

Lord, help me to flourish in Words!

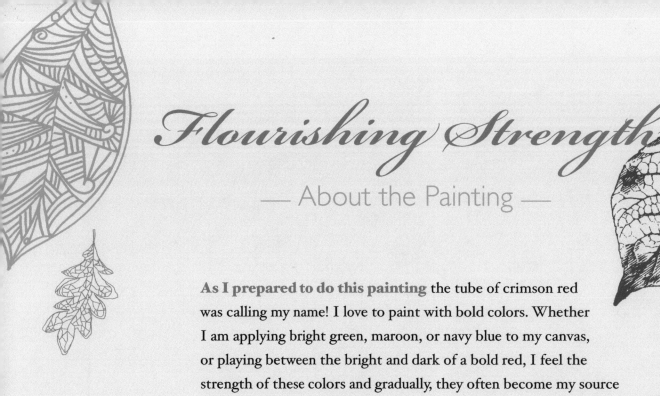

Flourishing Strength

— About the Painting —

As I prepared to do this painting the tube of crimson red was calling my name! I love to paint with bold colors. Whether I am applying bright green, maroon, or navy blue to my canvas, or playing between the bright and dark of a bold red, I feel the strength of these colors and gradually, they often become my source of inspiration. I love how the woman in the painting seems to be pushing her way out of a storm. She is determined to make her way across and find a sunny sky. My hope is that my painting gives you strength and inspires you to be bold yet kind and loving!

— Pause and Reflect —

What thoughts come to mind as you observed the colors, textures, movement, and emotion in the painting?

Flourishing Strength

After months of struggling with joint pain and generalized weakness, I finally made an appointment to see my doctor. When she entered the room she asked, "So what's the problem?" My response was, "Do you have a bucket?" Puzzled she looked up at me while I made a large circle with my arms and added, "So I can dump all my problems!" She laughed out loud, then I added, "No, seriously!" Then a few days later I fell and broke my left hand! Because I'm left handed, that complicates life, especially since I'm a writer. This was definitely not a season of strength for me,

and I was feeling rather discouraged. How on earth would I manage all my daily chores and responsibilities (cooking, cleaning, caring for my family. . .) with only one hand? So here I am typing this devotional with one finger, feeling frustrated and weak, while trying to make sense the verse — "For when I am weak, then I am strong" (2 Corinthians 12:10). What does that really mean?

Dictionaries define weakness as: "The condition of lacking strength, a quality or feature regarded as a disadvantage or fault." I think God's definition might read like this: A condition of fragility which teaches us to rely on God. Not regarded as a fault, rather an asset which reveals the power of God in our lives. As I ponder the painting of the lady in red, I can't help but admire how she's leaning into the storm, pressing on, determined to reach her goal. I wonder where she finds her strength? Did you know that when a tropical storm comes and unleashes its mighty winds against the trees, the palm tree is usually the only one left standing? The palm tree will bend, even all the way to the ground, but it won't break. Do you know why? The roots of an average plant only go down a few feet, but the roots of a palm tree go down hundreds of yards in search of water. That's how we find flourishing strength, dear friend. As we seek God daily through His Word and prayer, our roots grow deeper and deeper into His love. Then, when the storms of life come (and they certainly will) we will have the strength, grace, and perseverance to help us weather the storm! I can almost hear the lady in red shout out and encouraging, "Amen. Press on girls. We can do this!" The Psalmist writes, "The Godly will flourish like the palm trees and **grow strong** like the cedars of Lebanon" (Psalm 92:12). Now that's the kind of strength I'd like to have! As I linger a moment longer observing the painting, my eye is drawn to the umbrella under which she's taking shelter. It's a perfect visual for the topic of flourishing strength. As we take shelter under the umbrella of His love, we find the strength to press on. So press on dear friend! Past the pain. Past the discouragement. You can do all things, when you rely on Christ for strength!

Well, I'm still struggling with pain and stuck in this cast for several more weeks. But as I rely on God, I can declare: Even with a broken wing I can FLY! Hallelujah! "For those who WAIT on the

Flourishing Strength

LORD will gain new strength; They will mount up with wings like eagles, They will run and not get tired, They will walk and not become weary" (Isaiah 40:31). Dear friend, whether you're in a cast with a broken bone, are dealing with depression, anxiety, or any other "weakness," please hold onto these words from our beloved Savior— "My grace is sufficient for you, for My power is made perfect in weakness" (2 Corinthians 12:9). Flourishing Strength is therefore simply allowing God to shoulder our weaknesses, until His strength becomes our own! I've learned so much since my fall. I've learned to plant my roots deep into God's love (the true source of strength) for daily encouragement. I've also learned that no storm is without purpose and that ALL things (including my broken hand) are working for my good (Romans 8:28). One of the hardest lessons to learn, however, was simply to ask for help. Thank God for all those who help the hurting. They are the hands and feet of Jesus infusing strength and hope into the weak and wounded parts of humanity so that together we can declare with confidence— I can do all things through Christ who gives me strength (Philippians 4:13), to the glory of God. Amen.

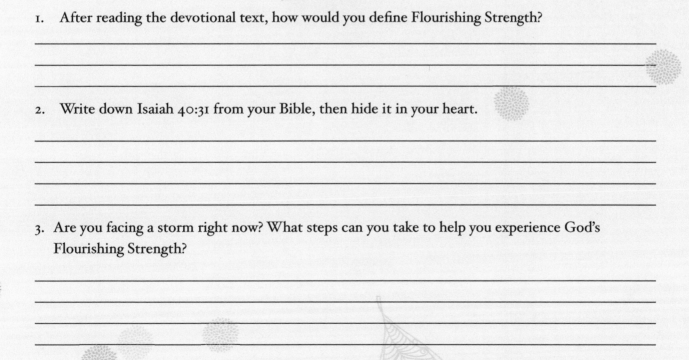

1. After reading the devotional text, how would you define Flourishing Strength?

_____
_____
_____

2. Write down Isaiah 40:31 from your Bible, then hide it in your heart.

_____
_____
_____
_____

3. Are you facing a storm right now? What steps can you take to help you experience God's Flourishing Strength?

_____
_____
_____
_____

It's time to color and journal your flourishing thoughts!

Flourishing Strength

*The Godly will flourish like
the palm trees and grow strong
like the cedars of Lebanon.*
—Psalm 92:12

Journal your flourishing thoughts about Strength.

_____
_____
_____
_____
_____
_____
_____
_____
_____
_____
_____
_____
_____
_____
_____
_____
_____

*I can do everything
through Christ
who gives me
strength.*
—Philippians 4:13

Lord, help me to flourish in Strength!

Flourishing Joy

— About the Painting —

Darkness surrounds the woman in the painting.

But look at her arms raised high!

I painted the red birds flying away

representing her "letting go" of her sadness.

There's always a glimmer of joy within us,

wanting to overcome the sadness.

Jesus placed it there!

That glimmer of joy is like a secret door,

that when opened ever so slightly through surrender and praise,

lets in torrents of light in to illuminate our soul.

The woman in the painting has found her joy!

— Pause and Reflect —

*What thoughts come to mind as you observed
the colors, textures, movement, and emotion in the painting?*

Flourishing Joy

It's safe to say that joy is something we all long for. There's something about having a joyful spirit that infuses strength into our being. And who doesn't need strength . . . strength to fight for your marriage, your health, or a child who's gone astray? The Bible says that the joy of the Lord is

my strength! (Nehemiah 8:10). I whole-heartedly agree, but for some reason, it's often one of the hardest emotions to experience. Yet God's Word tells us to "Rejoice Always!" (I Thessalonians 5:16). Is this really possible? It certainly is, my friend! But we have an enemy that would like us to think otherwise, and if he can steal our joy, then he can rob our strength and render us useless for God's Kingdom. But no more! JOY is one of the nine fruits of the Spirit, and it's your inheritance as a child of God. Are you ready to claim it?

Years ago I struggled with feelings of depression. I'm not exaggerating when I say, it felt like "living hell." Thus began my quest for joy. What I discovered was that joy, according to the Bible, is not the same as happiness. Happiness is based on circumstances, and is often fleeting. Joy however, is a posture of the heart, not based on our circumstances, but rather on the promises of God. Observe the painting of the lady in red for a moment. Do you see her surroundings? It's as if she's standing on the moon, a place void of life, dark and lonely. Now look at her posture . . . she's standing tall, arms raised, as if praising God despite her surroundings. Wouldn't it be nice to have this same posture no matter what trials come our way? But how? Joy, like all the fruits of the Spirit found in Galatians 5, comes as we abide in Christ. Abiding in Christ simply means to nurture and maintain our love relationship with Him. Hear His words: "I have loved you even as the Father has loved me. Remain in my love. When you obey my commandments, you remain in my love, just as I obey my Father's commandments and remain in His love. I have told you these things so that you will be filled with my joy. Yes, your joy will overflow!" (John 15:9-11). Abiding in Christ is how to receive Joy, but what does it look like in daily life?

In looking at the painting again, I'm kind of glad that we can't see her face. The faces of joy come in all shapes and sizes. Some people can smile, laugh, and appear "normal" during difficult times as they trust in God, while other believers have a hard time expressing those emotions. When I struggled with depression, I don't think I smiled much, and if I did, it was probably forced. But I had a peace that surpassed my understanding because I continued to read God's Word and trust in His promises. That gave me hope, strength, and even joy! What a paradox—a depressed joyful person! Only with God is this possible, and within that same year I was completely set free! Please hear me dear friend. God didn't promise us a trouble-free life, but He did promise to be with us. You must hold onto Jesus. He is the source of joy. NO amount of alcohol, drugs, relationships, chocolate, or any other comfort foods can bring you the joy that will sustain you through the valley. Psalm 16:11 tells us that in God's presence is fullness of joy! Can you imagine . . . FULLNESS OF JOY! So rather than focusing on your problems,

Flourishing Joy

come into God's presence, and trade sorrow for joy. When I'm feeling down I often read and pray the Psalms. It's the perfect place to "dump" the negative stuff, and you'll see that you're not alone. Read Psalm 13 and 18 for examples. The book of Philippians also has much to say about joy, and the writer, Paul, wrote it from his prison cell!

> Rejoice in the Lord always. I will say it again: Rejoice! . . . The Lord is near. Do not be anxious about anything, but in every situation, by prayer and petition, with thanksgiving, present your requests to God. And the peace of God, which transcends all understanding, will guard your hearts and your minds in Christ Jesus. Finally, brothers and sisters, whatever is true, whatever is noble, whatever is right, whatever is pure, whatever is lovely, whatever is admirable—if anything is excellent or praiseworthy—think about such things.

I wonder if Heaven has a special garden by the name of "joy"? I bet that each time we choose to praise God or give thanks during difficult times, Heaven's winds blow across that garden sending down petals of joy into our life. All we need to do is open our arms, like the girl the painting, and receive. Joy is therefore a supernatural gift from God, and when we express it despite our circumstances, it points people to God. Your friends may be wondering, "How on earth can you look okay, and even glow, with all that's happened to you?" And you'll respond with a glimmer in your eye, "Ah, it's not easy for sure. But the joy of the Lord is my strength!"

1. After reading the devotional text, how would you define Flourishing Joy?

_____

_____

_____

2. Write down Psalm 16:11 from your Bible, then hide it in your heart.

_____

_____

_____

3. Read James 1:2-3. According to this passage, troubles are an opportunity for great joy. Why do you think that is?

_____

_____

_____

It's time to color and journal your flourishing thoughts!

Flourishing Joy

Even though the fig trees have no blossoms,
and there are no grapes on the vines;
even though the olive crop fails,
and the fields lie empty and barren;
even though the flocks die in the fields,
and the cattle barns are empty,
yet I will rejoice in the Lord!
I will be joyful in the God of my salvation!
The Sovereign Lord is my strength!
He makes me as surefooted as a deer,
able to tread upon the heights.

—Habakkuk 3:17-19

Journal your flourishing thoughts about Joy.

_____

_____

_____

_____

_____

_____

_____

_____

_____

_____

Always be full of joy
in the Lord. I say it
again—rejoice!
—Philippians 4:4

Lord, help me to flourish in Joy!

Flourishing Healing

I drew the original sketch for this painting at church. In small letters next to the drawing I wrote: In oneness with Him—"Union of God and man." I suppose these words were from the sermon that day. One thing is for sure. When we are in oneness with God, we experience hope and tremendous healing! That's in essence what this painting represents. The more we look at her we stop seeing how fragile she seems and we start looking at how she glows!

— Pause and Reflect —

What thoughts come to mind as you observed
the colors, textures, movement, and emotion in the painting?

Flourishing Healing

When I first looked at the painting symbolizing Flourishing Healing, I immediately connected with the lady in red. Do you notice how she's looking over her shoulder gazing downward and away from the warm glow of light? Her shoulders are also rounded and her arms are lifted towards her chest. That was me, years ago. After a series of disappointing events I found myself weighed down by burdens, on my knees, and covering my wounded heart as if trying to protect myself from further pain.

Each morning I'd wake up with the same ache in my chest and wonder, "Will my heart ever heal?"

I've heard it said that from all the ailments a person can experience, a broken heart takes the longest to heal. Recently I broke my hand. The doctor gave me a clear diagnosis and said I'd be healed in 4 to 6 weeks. That gave me hope! A broken heart is a whole other story and we're often left feeling stuck in an endless cycle of pain! Every one of us has suffered at some point in our lives, whether physically or emotionally. It's the reality of living in a fallen world. Thankfully, there's no wound too deep for God to heal! He is the Great Physician and longs to mend our broken hearts. And whether He heals us today, in 4 to 6 weeks, or in a year, we can rest assured that ALL things are working for our good (Romans 8:28). The best part is that while we're healing we will be closer to God than ever before— "The LORD is close to the brokenhearted; he rescues those whose spirits are crushed" (Psalm 34:18). I've experienced firsthand the closeness of God during those times. God gently took my hand while together we worked through the mending process. That's what healing is. It's the process of becoming healthy and whole again. This process involves entrusting ourselves into the skilled hands of our Physician while He helps us to let go of the past, forgive, and to flourish in our faith. Of course, God could choose to heal us instantaneously. But more often than not He takes us on a journey and entrusts us with precious jewels of wisdom along the way!

Dear friend, please know that God truly cares for you and that no pain is without purpose. Your new heart will be stronger, wiser, more compassionate and loving than ever before! "Dear brothers and sisters, when troubles of any kind come your way, consider it an opportunity for great joy. For you know that when your faith is tested, your endurance has a chance to grow. So let it grow, for when your endurance is fully developed, you will be perfect and complete, needing nothing" (James 1:2-4). Can you imagine a heart, once broken, but now perfect and complete and lacking nothing? Hold onto that vision, and let the healing begin!

The image of the girl looking away, wounded, and on her knees, is no longer how I see myself. God's healing balm has come into my heart and made me whole, and life is so beautiful! Please don't let another precious moment go by with hurt in your heart. Look at the painting again. Do you notice the whimsical dragonflies fluttering around her head and the warm glow of light filtering in before her? It's almost as if the dragonflies are whispering encouraging words to her weary soul . . . "Come, my Beloved. Exchange your hurt for healing. Come out of darkness into God's marvelous healing light."

Flourishing Healing

The Spirit of God, the Master, is on me
because God anointed me.
He sent me to preach good news to the poor,
heal the heartbroken,
Announce freedom to all captives,
pardon all prisoners.
God sent me to announce the year of his grace—
a celebration of God's destruction of our enemies—
and to comfort all who mourn,
To care for the needs of all who mourn in Zion,
give them bouquets of roses instead of ashes,
Messages of joy instead of news of doom,
a praising heart instead of a languid spirit.
Rename them "Oaks of Righteousness"
planted by God to display his glory.
They'll rebuild the old ruins,
raise a new city out of the wreckage.
They'll start over on the ruined cities,
take the rubble left behind and make it new.

—Isaiah 61:1-7 The Message

1. After reading the devotional text, how would you define Flourishing Healing?

_____
_____

2. Write down Proverbs 4:23 from your Bible, then hide it in your heart.

_____
_____
_____
_____

3. What do you think it means to "guard your heart"?

_____
_____
_____
_____
_____
_____

It's time to color and journal your flourishing thoughts!

Flourishing Healing

Don't be impressed with your own wisdom. Instead, fear the LORD and turn away from evil. Then you will have healing for your body and strength for your bones.

—Proverbs 3:7-8

Journal your flourishing thoughts about Healing.

_____

_____

_____

_____

_____

_____

_____

_____

_____

_____

_____

Guard your heart above all else, for it determines the course of your life.

—Proverbs 4:23

Lord, help me to flourish in Healing!

Flourishing Wisdom

— About the Painting —

Looking at the calming blues and serene composition of this painting, you probably couldn't guess that I painted her while there was a ton of people all around me . . . sipping wine and enjoying live performances. Somehow I felt calm and kept painting for hours! It was almost as if I was in my own world. I knew exactly how she was going to look like once I was going to be done. I felt guided in creating my painting and I had a vision in my mind. Wouldn't it be great to live our lives feeling guided, like a paintbrush in the hands of a skillful artist? Well, as Christians we can feel that way . . . trust God and keep your faith! Pray for guidance and remember to pause and quiet your life often!

— Pause and Reflect —

What thoughts come to mind as you observed the colors, textures, movement, and emotion in the painting?

Flourishing Wisdom

Years ago, my children and I were hooked on Disney. We still are actually! One night after their bath, all comfy cozy in our PJ's, we snuggled together on the sofa to watch *Sleeping Beauty*. I was intrigued by the scene where six of the seven fairies offer their gifts to the infant Princess at her Christening—beauty, wit, grace, dance, song, and goodness. I couldn't help but wonder why none of the fairies gave her the gift of wisdom! It would seem to be a most worthy gift. Even God's Word tells us "how much better to get wisdom than gold!" (Proverbs 16:16). That same night I decided to ask God for specific gifts for my children. Yes, Disney inspired me! I thought of gifts that the Bible holds in the highest regard. Wisdom and Love came to mind. I thought if my children had these two

gifts, everything else in life would fall into place and their life choices would be pleasing to God.

Interestingly, at the moment we accept Christ as our Savior, we also become daughters of the most high. In other words, we become a Princess! And while God doesn't send fairies to endow us with precious gifts, He does send His Holy Spirit to teach us how to access all that Heaven has to offer, including the wisdom from above. I don't know about you, but I could sure use a daily dose of God's wisdom. I struggle with decision-making, and often ask God for guidance. Fortunately, His wisdom is not hidden. It's revealed within the pages of scripture and works like a lighthouse guiding us through the storms of life.

I love the painting Nathalie did with the lady sitting by the water reading. I immediately noticed the lighthouse in the background and thought of this verse: "Your word is a lamp to guide my feet and a light for my path" (Psalm 119:105). I imagined myself sitting by the still waters reading my Bible and being guided by God's light. I've honestly never experienced anything like it. While reading and meditating on God's Word, it's as if a still small voice whispers, come this way, or go that way. For years I thought that in order to gain "wisdom," I had to learn more, read more, gain more knowledge, and experience life to the fullest. While those things are all helpful, they do no grant us access to God's wisdom. "The fear of the LORD is the beginning of wisdom" (Proverbs 9:10). Wisdom begins when we submit our heart to God in reverent fear. That is when we gain access to the wisdom from above, which is often the exact opposite of how we feel. "But the wisdom from above is first of all pure. It is also peace-loving, gentle at all times, and willing to yield to others. It is full of mercy and good deeds. It shows no favoritism and is always sincere" (James 3:17). **Gaining** wisdom is so important that almost an entire book of the Bible (Proverbs) is dedicated to the topic.

After taking what seems like a million wrong turns in life, I've come to cherish the wisdom from God's Word more than anything. When dense fog clouds my thoughts and ability to make decisions, or when the storms of life cause me to feel anxious or fearful, God's Word shines as a beacon of light

Flourishing Wisdom

guiding me safely to shore! Dear friend, I realize that we live in a fast-food society and we often expect access to food and everything else quickly and easily. But there are no short cuts to gaining the wisdom from above. Even a seed doesn't magically transform into a flourishing plant overnight. It needs fertile soil, sunshine, and water. In the same way, we need the nourishment of God's Word to gain the wisdom needed to go through life. Read, pray, and ASK God for wisdom daily (James 1:5). He loves to help! After years of being tossed to and fro seeking signs and experiences to guide me, and being constantly confused and disappointed, my prayer is now: "Dear God, please don't speak to me through heartache or blessing. Speak to me through Your Word. I desperately need YOUR wisdom. May it be the guiding light in all I do. In Jesus name, Amen."

For you, the Eternal's Word is your happiness. It is your focus—from dusk to dawn. You are like a tree, planted by flowing, cool streams of water that never run dry. Your fruit ripens in its time; your leaves never fade or curl in the summer sun. No matter what you do, you prosper.
—Psalm 1:2-3 The Voice

1. After reading the devotional text, how would you describe Flourishing Wisdom?
_____
_____

2. Write down James 1:5 from your Bible, then hide it in your heart.
_____
_____
_____
_____

3. In what areas of your life do you need God's wisdom?
_____
_____
_____
_____
_____
_____
_____

It's time to color and journal your flourishing thoughts!

Flourishing Wisdom

But the wisdom from above is first of all pure. It is also peace loving, gentle at all times, and willing to yield to others. It is full of mercy and the fruit of good deeds. It shows no favoritism and is always sincere.

—James 3:17

Journal your flourishing thoughts about Wisdom.

How much better to get wisdom than gold!
—Proverbs 16:16

Lord, help me to flourish in Wisdom!

Flourishing Peace

Acceptance drains away worry, fear, and anxiety. It is the door to our peace. The woman in the painting is accepting and receiving the Holy Spirit. Her hands are open and she is willing to go through the storms of life with God's peace. See how the flowers on the right of the painting are going from black to gold? These blooms represent the transformation within her soul as she accepts God's peace. Make a cup with your hands and bring your hands to your heart. Now say, "The doors of my heart are open to your will and your love, Lord, Amen."

— Pause and Reflect —

*What thoughts come to mind as you observed
the colors, textures, movement, and emotion in the painting?*

Flourishing Peace

There are really only three things I need to know about life: God has my best interest at heart, God loves me, and God is good. No matter what I'm going through, if I have these three things, I have peace. The problem is, the enemy is constantly trying to get me to doubt God in one or all of these

three areas. It happened to me a few years ago during our move from the west coast to the east. For those who don't know, moving is on the top ten list of life stressors! Thankfully, my dogs felt otherwise, and they taught me an important lesson.

During our stressful five-day trek moving across the country, I noticed something very interesting. While I was frazzled and fretting, and trying to digest leaving everything that was familiar, my dogs were sleeping peacefully, eating well, and ready to play fetch each time we stopped to stretch our legs. I realized that for them, I was their stable force—the assurance that all would go well. As long as they could see me and snuggle close, they were content, despite having their routine disrupted and being crammed into a tiny RV. Their example caused me to wonder: Did I really believe that God was with me while my life was being turned upside down? Why wasn't I able to relax and enjoy the journey? If you've ever taken a long road trip, one thing is for sure, you never really know what lies ahead. There could be traffic jams, accidents, harsh weather conditions, as well as peaceful scenery and fun times. "Not knowing" what the future holds can bring an element of anxiety, unless we know who is with us . . . and I don't mean our spouse, or our girl friends. They can be a comfort, but only God knows what lies ahead. Faith assures us that although we cannot see Him, nor what's down the road in life, **God is with us.**

As I prepare to color the painting symbolizing *Flourishing Peace,* I can't help but notice the soul-searching posture of the lady on her knees, reaching out as if she's welcoming the dove. When we receive Jesus as our Savior we also receive the Holy Spirit (symbolized in the dove), and with it the potential to experience all the fruits of the Holy Spirit, one of which is peace— "And the fruit of the Spirit is love, joy, peace . . ." (Galatians 5:22-23). Do you notice what the dove is carrying? The olive branch is a symbol of peace. That olive branch is for you, my friend! Will you receive it today? Jesus said— "I am leaving you with a gift—peace of mind and heart. And the peace I give is a gift the world cannot give. So don't be troubled or afraid" (John 14:27).

Dear friend, I know that it's easy to lose our peace. We worry about so many things—what we look like, what we will wear, and what others may think of us. There are also worries about the future—how will we pay for college, our medical bills, or make the house payments? The enemy knows our weak spots and sneaks in to tempt us to doubt God. If he succeeds in sowing doubt in our hearts, peace cannot flourish. That's why it's so important to stay close to God through His Word, prayer, praise and worship, as well as fellowship with the body of Christ. God is the source of peace. **He is peace.**

Flourishing Peace

The closer we draw to Him, the more peace we will experience. Just like my doggies who snuggled close to me for comfort during our stressful journey, you too can snuggle up close to God and receive a quietness of spirit that transcends your understanding. That's when peace flourishes, my friend. Like the petals of a flowers unfolding in the morning sunlight, the petals of peace unfold in our lives as we draw close to God. He is the secret garden in our hearts that we can run to. Those who look to Him are radiant (Psalm 34), and their hearts are filled with peace!

What I learned during the long trek from west coast to east, thanks to my dogs' constant focus on me, was that I can fix my eyes on my fears about the future, or I can fix my eyes on my Savior. It's simply a choice. The last night of our trip, as I curled up with my dogs to sleep, I chose to place my trust and focus fully on God, and guess what? His Word is true! Isaiah 26:3 tells us that God will keep in **perfect peace** all who **trust** in Him, all whose thoughts are **fixed** on Him. So the next time the enemy tries to steal your peace, just remember: God has your best interest at heart, God loves you, and God is sooooo good! Focusing on these three things along life's journey is all you need to experience God's peace.

May the peace of God, which transcends all understanding, guard your hearts and minds in Christ Jesus!

—Philippians 4:7

1. After reading the devotional text, how would you receive Flourishing Peace?
    _____
    _____

2. Write down Philippians 4:6-9 from your Bible, then hide it in your heart.
    _____
    _____
    _____
    _____
    _____

3. According to Philippians 4:6-9, what specific things can you do daily to receive God's peace?
    _____
    _____
    _____
    _____

It's time to color and journal your flourishing thoughts!

Flourishing Peace

You will keep in perfect peace
all who trust in you,
all whose thoughts are fixed on you!
—Isaiah 26:3

Journal your flourishing thoughts about Peace.

_____

_____

_____

_____

_____

_____

_____

_____

_____

_____

_____

_____

_____

_____

The Lord gives his
people strength.
The Lord blesses
them with peace.
—Psalm 29:11

Lord, help me to flourish in Peace!

Flourishing Prayer

I painted this woman praying and kneeling on a rock to represent how the key image for the Lord is a "Rock." He is OUR Rock. This painting speaks of His stability in a changing world and His dependability in a demanding world. The Rock is our Saviour, our Father, and our Deliverer. He is all we need. Dear friend, pray to the Rock and do not be worried. May God cause us all to grow in faith until we pray without ceasing (1 Thessalonians 5:17) and never lose heart (Luke 18:1).

— Pause and Reflect —

What thoughts come to mind as you observed the colors, textures, movement, and emotion in the painting?

Flourishing Prayer

Have you ever prayed for something so long that you eventually became discouraged and began to doubt that anything would change? For several years I've had chronic shoulder pain. Lifting, carrying, or anything that required full range of motion in my shoulder was agonizing. Despite

doctor visits and prayers, it only seemed to get worse. Resting it was probably the only solution, but that wasn't possible, due to my work. So I continued to pray, but as the months and years went by, I became discouraged. I wondered, "Was God listening? Was God even up there?" And of course the "Why Me?" question had to come up. Maybe you've been there?

During that season I tried to encourage myself with verses such as Philippians 4:6, "Don't worry about anything; instead, pray about everything. Tell God what you need, and thank him for all he has done." So I poured out my heart to God, but as time passed, my sweet, heartfelt, fervent prayers turned sour. Then something happened that really pushed my buttons. I fell and broke my hand. After crying awhile and feeling sorry for myself, all I could think to pray was, "REALLY GOD!?!"

Thankfully I got hold of my emotions and was encouraged by friends and family to wait and trust in God's unseen plan. A few weeks later, while still in my cast, it suddenly dawned on me . . . my shoulder no longer hurt! I realized that the enforced rest due to being in a cast must have been the reason. In that instant these words flashed across my mind: "My beloved child, I allowed your hand to break so that I could heal your shoulder. I work ALL things for good." WOW, God heard all my prayers, dried every tear, and was working behind the scenes all along! I sat in silent wonder, my thoughts drifting back to the time I danced in a ballet company. I recalled all the intricacies that went on behind the scenes to prepare for opening night. The dancers, costume makers, stage hands, musicians, and so many others worked hard for months to create a magnificent work or art. I imagine God saying to each one of us as we pray, "Patience, my child. I'm working behind the scenes, and I won't open the curtain until everything is in place and ready."

I love the painting of the girl kneeling by a rock. She represents each one of us, earnestly coming before the Lord with our petitions. When I first saw the painting I only saw her. But then I noticed the colors gathering into a warm glow right around her head pointing me to the rock. That is who we are coming to in prayer, Jesus Christ—He is our Rock (Psalm 18:2), our firm foundation and focus in an ever changing world! So stand firm and trust in God's promises. One day, that curtain will rise, and you'll be able to declare, "And we know that God causes everything to work together for the good of those who love God and are called according to his purpose for them" (Romans 8:28).

Flourishing Prayer

One final word of encouragement: I Thessalonians 5:17 tells us to pray without ceasing. I used to think this was impossible. How does one pray non-stop? I think this verse is simply telling us to invite God into every nook and cranny of our life until prayer becomes as natural as breathing. So breathe in, my friend, and invite God into all you do. Let prayer become your ongoing conversation with your Heavenly Father (with or without words), and never give up. God loves you and is meticulously working behind the scenes. . . for your good, and for His glory! Amen.

I love the LORD because he hears my voice and my prayer for mercy.
Because he bends down to listen, I will pray as long as I have breath!

—Luke 22:42

1. After reading the devotional text, how would you define Flourishing Prayer?
_____
_____

2. Jesus gave us a model for prayer in Matthew 6:9-13. Write these verses from your Bible, then hide them in your heart.
_____
_____
_____
_____
_____
_____
_____
_____

3. According to Hebrews 4:16, how are we to approach God when we pray? Why do you think that is?
_____
_____
_____
_____
_____
_____
_____
_____

It's time to color and journal your flourishing thoughts!

Flourishing Prayer

Don't worry about anything; instead,
pray about everything.
Tell God what you need, and
thank Him for all He has done.

—*Philippians 4:6*

Journal your flourishing thoughts about Prayer.

_____

_____

_____

_____

_____

_____

_____

_____

_____

_____

_____

_____

_____

Devote yourselves
to prayer with an
alert mind and
a thankful heart.
—*Colossians 4:2*

Lord, help me to flourish in Prayer!

Flourishing Courage

She climbs up the steep hill,

overcoming many obstacles on her path.

She reaches for courage within herself

Knowing it's a gift from God.

Her friend is struggling behind her, thinking,

"I can't do this, the path is too hard. I'm not strong enough."

She extends her hand to help her and reassures her saying,

"You can do this. Follow me. I'll help you face the challenges.

Together we will be the fearless women God intended us to be!"

— Pause and Reflect —

What thoughts come to mind as you observed
the colors, textures, movement, and emotion in the painting?

Flourishing Courage

Often at night, Laura and Lisa would sit at their father's feet listening to the stories of his life as a mountain guide in the Alps. The young twins were enthralled by the way he described the mountain, so powerful and majestic. They could almost see the snowy peak and the view from the top reflecting in

his eyes as he spoke. His 25 years up there gave him many stories to tell, filled with excitement, adventure, and even danger! Year after year their desire to climb the mountain grew, and they begged him to take them to the peak. The day finally came that he agreed. It was their dream come true!

As they approached the mountain they all paused and gazed at its awesomeness. The snowy peak looked so pure and inviting from the distance, yet so far. Laura took a deep breath to calm her nerves. Fearful by nature, she felt so small and a bit anxious facing the ominous mountain ahead. "Father," she asked, "Are you sure we can do this? What if a bear attacks us or we get tired and faint with no one to rescue us?" Her father smiled. "It's normal to feel scared," he said. "It's a long journey ahead, but I will be with you and guide you safely to the top, don't worry."

Reassured by her father's words, she held his hand and continued on. Lisa, the adventurous type, took little thought for the hike, walking at a brisk pace ahead and enjoying the sunny mountain views. As it was getting dark their father led them to a shelter, started a fire, and encouraged them to get a good night's rest.

They arose early to the sound of heavy rain, not feeling as enthusiastic as the day before. The father awoke happily, not bothered by the rain. He made a warm breakfast and urged them on their way saying, "Stay behind me and close enough to follow in my footsteps. The trail ahead is narrow, and there are many loose rocks." Laura took each step slowly and carefully, keeping an eye on her father, but Lisa pushed ahead not heeding her father's advice. Suddenly, Lisa slipped on a rock and fell into a deep crevice. Hurt and frightened and unable to pull herself out, she screamed for help. It seemed like an eternity before her father and Laura were able to find her and throw a rope to pull her up. Lying there aching from head to toe, she tucked her head into her father's arms and apologized saying that she loved him. "I know you love me," replied her father, "but show it by obeying my advice. I love you, and it breaks my heart when you hurt yourself." The next day, as they approached the peak, their arms and legs burned with pain and they worried that they wouldn't make it to the top. Their father, knowing their thoughts, got out a rope to keep them connected, making sure he would be able to catch them in case they became fainthearted or slipped. He'd never in his 25 years as guide lost a traveler!

Finally they arrived, all gazing in silent wonder. The peak seemed so magical, white, spotless, and pure, with no footprints. Laura began to cry tears of joy. She had been so scared along the journey, but now she felt so free, so happy! Her sister however stood silent. "What are you thinking?" her father asked. Lisa remembered the day she disobeyed her father's advice and slipped, almost losing her life. She

Flourishing Courage

realized how sad it would have been to miss this magnificent view and experience the joy. Her father, knowing her thoughts, simply hugged her and said, "I love you so much, my child!" Then he lovingly gathered the twins by his side and said, "Now you understand why I had to guide you. I knew that the journey would be long and hard, and that it would take courage and perseverance to make it to the top. The courage to achieve your dream was possible because you walked with me and trusted me to help you. You see now that courage is not the absence of fear, it's the choice to persevere despite the difficulties you face, knowing that I am with you always."

One last thought about the painting. We don't see the "father" with the two girls, yet we trust he is there leading the way. Life is so similar. While we cannot see God ahead of us on life's journey, knowing He is there gives us the courage to press on. Sometimes we may even need a sister or brother in Christ to help us along, as shown in the painting. Are you facing a mountain, i.e. a difficult decision, fear, injustice, persecution? Stay close to Jesus, my friend, take His hand, and let His truth guide your every step. Courage comes as you trust in Him. Let's encourage each other with these words:

So be strong and courageous! Do not be afraid and do not panic before them. For the Lord your God will personally go ahead of you. He will neither fail you nor abandon you.

—Deuteronomy 31:6

1. After reading the devotional text, how would you define Flourishing Courage?

_____

_____

_____

2. Write down Psalm 56:3 from your Bible, then hide it in your heart.

_____

_____

_____

_____

_____

3. According to Psalm 56:3, how do we get courage when we feel afraid?

_____

_____

_____

_____

It's time to color and journal your flourishing thoughts!

Flourishing Courage

This is my command—
be strong and courageous!
Do not be afraid or discouraged.
For the Lord your God
is with you wherever you go.
—Joshua 1:9

Journal your flourishing thoughts about Courage.

_____

_____

_____

_____

_____

_____

_____

_____

_____

_____

_____

_____

When I am afraid,
I will put my trust
in you.
—Psalm 56:3

Lord, help me to flourish in Courage!

Flourishing Freedom

I painted a woman leaping through the air and twirling her pretty silk. As I took a few steps back to look at my painting, I noticed how I painted her with such lightness and abandon. For a few seconds I wanted to become her! Beautiful music was playing on the radio so I let my free spirit take over and attempted a few spins. Still holding my paintbrush in my hand I kept smiling as I added a few more flowers on her pretty silk.

— Pause and Reflect —

What thoughts come to mind as you observed the colors, textures, movement, and emotion in the painting?

Flourishing Freedom

Early one morning while jogging along a trail covered in autumn leaves, I sensed God saying, "Run, my child, run, run, you are free!" As I ran, an image came to mind of chains falling off, one by one, allowing me to run with even more ease and freedom. Times I'd felt chained to worries, fear, and the painful memories of a broken heart flashed across my mind, but rather than feeling the usual heaviness of heart, I felt so light! Tears of joy ran down my face and an overwhelming sense of gratitude filled my heart. I knew that season of my life was now in the past, and like the falling leaves all around me those chains were falling behind as I ran. A gentle breeze brushed across my face whispering, "So if the Son sets you free, you are truly free" (John 8:36). What does it mean to be "free in Christ"? Is it being able to do whatever you want? In what sense does Christ make us free? Ironically, the word freedom when used in scripture and Christian tradition holds a very different meaning from our cultural understanding of freedom.

The definition of freedom from a cultural and human point of view simply means to have the right to think, speak, and act as we want without hindrance. Everyone wants these freedoms, but true freedom (spiritually speaking) is the absence of chains and can only be found within the context of servitude to God. The word *doulos*, which is mentioned 124 times in the New Testament, means "someone who belongs to another" or "bond-slave with no ownership rights of his own." It's used throughout scripture to explain our relationship to Christ. But why would Christ want to enslave us to Himself? Here's an analogy to help us understand. Imagine a train rolling along on the tracks. It's freely moving forward towards its destination. Now imagine the train coming off the track. It's still free, but now it's heading for destruction. Being tethered to those tracks ensures its safety. In the same way, being tethered to Christ as a bond-slave ensures a safe arrival to our final destination, Heaven. Only He knows what's best for us, which is why we need to give up "our rights" and entrust our lives fully to His Lordship. Someone might argue, "But no one owns me!" But according to Romans 6, no one is free—we are either slaves to sin, or slaves to righteousness, and the Bible tells us that we must choose whom we will serve. Following our fleshly desires may feel good and seem easy in the moment, but Proverbs 14:12 warns us that "there is a path before each person that seems right, but it ends in death." Standing in stark contrast, Jesus unfolds before us a different path— "the path of life." This road leads to true freedom and eternal life with God. It's not an easy one, however (Matthew 7:14), which is why it's so important to travel light. According to Hebrews 12:1, we must throw off every weight that slows us down from pursuing Christ. When I take off on a walk or jog, I carry nothing (except water) and I dress light! Traveling light allows me the freedom to run with ease.

Traveling light . . . what a beautiful concept to go along with the topic of Flourishing Freedom! Look at the painting for a moment, doesn't the girl appear light and ethereal? It's as if she's been freed from a miry pit, from all her sin and shame, and she's flying up and up towards her destiny. For me, the scarf

Flourishing Freedom

she's holding is her garment of praise and she's leaping for joy to tell the world all that the Lord has done for her. What an appropriate testimony for the follower of Christ! I can almost hear her singing, "He lifted me out of the pit of despair, out of the mud and the mire. He set my feet on solid ground and steadied me as I walked along. He has given me a new song to sing, a hymn of praise to our God. Many will see what he has done and be amazed. They will put their trust in the Lord" (Psalm 40:1-2). Dear friend, the heights and joys of true freedom in Christ can only be experienced once our eyes are opened to the depths of our bondage without Him. That is why, although no one likes to talk about the shackles of sin, it's the only way to come to grips with our need for a Savior. Once we are set free, we can walk into newness of life through obedience and faith. Serving Him is never a burden, for it is with joy and thanksgiving that we offer our lives to the One who set us free from sin and death and offered us the hope of eternal life! I understand now that I am not my own, I've been bought with the precious blood of Christ and am set free for His purposes and glory! Now I can freely grow into the authentic person God created me to be, and you can too . . .

What chains are holding you back from running into your destiny with Christ? Fear of man, insecurity, shame, doubt or unbelief? Please don't wait. Flourishing freedom is only a prayer away. Luke 17:33 in *The Message* translation tells us that "if you grasp and cling to life on your terms, you'll lose it, but if you let that life go, you'll get life on God's terms." So let go, my friend, God's ways are so much better than ours. He wants you to experience true freedom in every area of your life!

> *For the Lord is the Spirit, and wherever the Spirit of the Lord is, there is freedom."*
> —2 Corinthians 3:17

1. After reading the devotional text, how would you describe Flourishing Freedom?

_____

_____

_____

2. Write down John 8:36 from your Bible, then hide it in your heart.

_____

_____

_____

_____

3. According to Hebrews 12:1, we must strip off every weight that slows us down. What weights do you feel are slowing you down from pursuing Christ?

_____

_____

_____

_____

It's time to color and journal your flourishing thoughts!

Flourishing Freedom

So Christ has truly set us free.
Now make sure that you stay free,
and don't get tied up again
in slavery to the law.
—Galatians 5:1

Journal your flourishing thoughts about Freedom.

So if the Son sets
you free, you are
truly free.
—John 8:36

Lord, help me to flourish in Freedom!

Flourishing Praise & Worship

— About the Painting —

The woman in this painting is worshiping God while playing beautiful music with her harp. Whether you play music, dance, sing, paint, or raise your arms really high, know that God loves it when we praise Him. Isn't it so comforting to know that we will never be too heavy for God to lift us up! We remain His little children and to Him, we are as light as feathers! Praise Him, worship Him and be lifted high!

— Pause and Reflect —

*What thoughts come to mind as you observed
the colors, textures, movement, and emotion in the painting?*

Flourishing Praise & Worship

Thunderous applause filled the auditorium and crescendoed into a standing ovation as the acclaimed dancers took their bows. Roses were thrown at their feet and I joined with the audience in

shouting "BRAVO, BRAVO!" I had an urge to run onto the stage, throw my arms around the dancers, and tell them how much I loved their performance! But of course I restrained my-self. The curtains closed and the dancers disappeared behind the scenes. That's what is called "praise." We can praise our family and friends, our favorite sports teams, musicians, and dancers. And of course our highest praise goes to our beloved Savior Jesus Christ. Thousands of years ago, another curtain closed. Actually, the curtain tore in half when Jesus Christ took his final breath and disappeared from the stage of life. But three days later, to the thunderous applause of angelic hosts, He rose again, forever making a way for us to approach God. Jesus suffered and died on the cross, taking on the penalty of our sin in order to reconcile us back to God and offer us eternal life. But what does that have to do with praise and worship you may ask? That one act of sacrificial love is the reason we stand up and shout, "You are worthy, O Lord our God, to receive glory and honor and power!" (Revelation 4:11). Praise is simply the truthful acknowledgment of the righteous acts of another, whether that be God, or our family or friends. Worship, on the other hand, is reserved for God alone (Exodus 20:3, Luke 4:8), and is shown by our deep reverence and expressions of love such as bowing and kneeling before Him. Let's take a closer look at these two powerful and meaningful words, praise and worship.

The act of "praising God" is really very personal, and is more a matter of the heart than what we do with our hands or voices. That said, scripture does give us numerous examples of people engaging in praise and worship. Psalm 150:4-6 gives a perfect illustration—"Praise him with the tambourine and dancing; praise him with strings and flutes! . . . Let everything that breathes sing praises to the Lord!" The painting representing Flourishing Praise and Worship also gives us a window into the heart of a worshiper. Everything about it speaks surrender, abandon, freedom, and extravagant love for God. Even the colors appear to be dancing on the canvas to the tune of the harp! The tiny silhouette of a woman in the top right corner of the painting, with the tambourine, reminds me of the prophetess Miriam from Exodus 15:20. I'd love to be like the Miriam, leading the women in dance, twirling with tambourine in hand—arms raised, eyes gazing heavenward in sweet surrender and praise to God. But it's not always easy to praise God. Often I'm held back by concern for what others may think, or dis-appointments and heartache that weigh my heart down. Maybe you can relate? Dear friend, we must never opt out of praise and worship based on our circumstances and feelings. It's the pathway to God's presence, power, and blessing. "Therefore, let us offer through Jesus a continual sacrifice of praise to God, proclaiming our allegiance to His name" (Hebrews 13:15).

Flourishing Praise & Worship

As we surrender our lives fully to God and call to mind all that He has done for us, the spotlight moves away from our idols and preoccupation with "self" and shines where it belongs, on Jesus Christ. I'm so thankful for Jesus, aren't you? Think back to the cross for a moment. What does the sacrifice of Christ stir within you? Are you inspired to give a standing ovation and shout out, "BRAVO, BRAVO!" to the one who delivered you from darkness, wiped your slate clean, and offered you a new life and the assurance of eternity with God? When I consider all that He's done for me, my heart is filled with thanksgiving, and I'm often moved to tears. Other times I feel compelled to raise my arms, twirl and sway, or kneel in silent wonder while soaking in some worship music. I'm so glad that I don't have to hold back my emotions with God, like I did at the ballet when I wanted to run on stage and embrace the dancers, but had to restrain myself. The curtain separating man and God has been torn in half, hallelujah! Now, I can come before His presence freely, and you can too, my friend (Psalm 100:4).

I'd like to encourage you to a "lifestyle" of praise and worship. David prayed, in Psalm 34:1, "I will praise the Lord at ALL times. I will continually speak his praise!" That means we can give ourselves permission to praise the Lord at any moment of the day or night, while at church, at home, or at play, and through every season of life. Let's offer our lives as instruments of praise and embrace our Lord with adoring hearts! Sing with me—"Let all that I am praise the Lord; with my whole heart, I will praise His Holy Name." (Psalm 103:1).

1. After reading the devotional text, how would you define Flourishing Praise and Worship?

_____
_____

2. Write down Psalm 103:1 from your Bible, then hide it in your heart.

_____
_____
_____

3. According to Psalm 103:1, we are to praise God with our whole heart. What are some specific ways you can do that while at church and during your daily activities?

_____
_____
_____

It's time to color and journal your flourishing thoughts!

Flourishing Praise & Worship

Let all that I am praise the Lord;
with my whole heart, I will praise his holy name.
Let all that I am praise the Lord;
may I never forget the good things he does for me.
He forgives all my sins
and heals all my diseases.
He redeems me from death
and crowns me with love and tender mercies.
He fills my life with good things.
My youth is renewed like the eagle's!
—Psalm 103:1-5

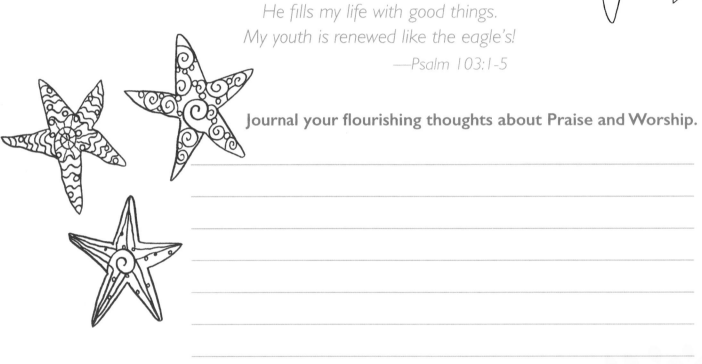

Journal your flourishing thoughts about Praise and Worship.

_____

_____

_____

_____

_____

_____

_____

_____

_____

_____

_____

_____

Oh come, let us worship and bow down; let us kneel before the Lord, our Maker!
—Psalm 95:6

Lord, help me to flourish in Praise and Worship!

Flourishing Love

— About the Painting —

A friend of mine came over for lunch and I told her
how much I loved a song called "Here's My Heart, Lord,"
by Lauren Daigle. She proposed we'd play the song and
worship. By the time the song was over, I created the
illustration that became the inspiration for this painting.
As I observed my drawing, I realized it was representing
a woman accepting Jesus as her Lord and Savior. When
I did the painting, I really wanted to express how God
showers us with His love the moment we accept Jesus in
our heart. I painted the rays gently cascading over her to
represents the joy we find in Him daily.

— Pause and Reflect —

*What thoughts come to mind as you observed
the colors, textures, movement, and emotion in the painting?*

Flourishing Love

Have you ever wondered why we were created with such a strong need for love? I believe that God placed within us one piece of a two-piece puzzle, and that it is only in Him that we become

complete and find our purpose and identity. Yet so many people are looking for that missing piece in all the wrong places. We look for love from our friends, parents, spouse, from our children, and even from our pets. But can any of these truly fulfill our need for love? Who can understand the depths of the human heart, except God? God is love (I John 4:8), and therefore love is found in the heart of God. He is that missing puzzle piece! Let's see what God says about love. . .

1 Corinthians 13:4-8, 13, says:

Love is patient, love is kind. It does not envy, it does not boast, it is not proud. It is not rude, it is not self-seeking, it is not easily angered, it keeps no record of wrongs. Love does not delight in evil but rejoices with the truth. It always protects, always trusts, always hopes, always perseveres. Love never fails . . . And now these three things remain: faith, hope and love. But the greatest of these is love.

As I read this I see how easy it can be to fall short, but I also see how our love grows, as we mature in our relationships with others and with God. It's a life-long process. But even then, love can be a confusing concept. It's a word that is widely used and often misunderstood. Let's look at the three meanings of love given to us in the Greek. *Eros* love relates to sexual love; it can be emotional as well. *Phileo* love describes a "brotherly love," and *Agape* love is a love that's given and expects no return. While all three aspects of love have their place, *Agape* love (demonstrated by Christ) is the most effective of these three in building a foundation for any lasting relationship. It also acts like an umbrella for which all other aspects of love exist. If we try to build a relationship based on *Eros* love alone, it will only last as long as the emotions felt or the sexual gratification. *Phileo* love will last as long as the person gives love in return. *Agape* love, on the other hand, will always last, because it expects nothing in return and has no conditions that come with it. This is how God loves us: unconditionally. It's that very love that draws us to Himself, and woos us until we surrender our lives to Him.

I was immediately touched by the painting representing Flourishing Love. What a perfect visual of coming to God in sweet surrender, offering Him our heart, and receiving His love in return. Three words came to my mind when I saw this painting—The Great Exchange! Picture kneeling before God and exchanging your old, weary, sinful heart for one that is brand new, spotless, and full of life! I made that exchange at the tender age of 16. Ever since, I feel His love deep within my soul and I know that no matter what comes my way, I am loved. That is all I ever wanted, and in Him, I am complete! If you'd like to make that great exchange, and experience God's love today, please take a

Flourishing Love

moment and pray this prayer. It's the first step to flourishing in any area of your life, because it is only as we abide in Christ that we find the love that we've always been looking for.

Dear Heavenly Father, I come to you today acknowledging my need for love. I also understand that I need a new heart, a new mind, and a new life. Please forgive me for my sin. I receive the free gift of salvation, offered through the perfect sacrifice of your Son Jesus Christ. Open my eyes to the love you have for me, and help me to share that love with others. Help me to walk with you, guided by the Holy Spirit, all the days of my life. Thank you for a new heart! In Jesus name, Amen.

Once you've prayed, turn to page 96 to learn more about the amazing faith-filled journey from seedling to flourishing plant. I can't tell you how excited I am to share this journey with you. All of Heaven rejoices when a child becomes aware of her adoption as a child of God!

1.   After reading the devotional text, how would you describe Flourishing Love?

_____
_____
_____

2.   Write down 1 Corinthians 13:13 from your Bible, then hide it in your heart.

_____
_____
_____
_____

3.   1 Corinthians 13:4-8 describes God's love. Choose one quality from that description in which you struggle. Commit that to prayer.

_____
_____
_____
_____

It's time to color and journal your flourishing thoughts!

Flourishing Love

'And you must love the Lord your God with all your
heart, all your soul, all your mind, and all your strength.'
The second is equally important:
'Love your neighbor as yourself.'
No other commandment is greater than these.

—Mark 12:30-31

Journal your flourishing thoughts about Love.

_____

_____

_____

_____

_____

_____

_____

_____

_____

_____

Three things will last
forever—faith, hope,
and love—and the
greatest of these
is love.
—1 Corinthians 13:13

Lord, help me to flourish in Love!

Steps to Flourishing in Faith
— The Journey Begins —

The journey from seedling to flourishing plant is a miraculous journey initiated by God and sustained by Him from start to finish. Once we become aware of His love for us, and our adoption as beloved sons and daughters of God, the journey begins! That's when the seed of faith God placed within us takes root and begins to flourish. These verses from God's Word share important truths about the journey . It is our earnest prayer that they'll help you to taste and see the goodness of God that you may know the height and breadth of His incredible love for you! We are so excited to share this journey with you dear friend! Are you ready to take that first step?

1. I acknowledge that I am separated from God due to my sin.

"All of us, like sheep, have strayed away. We have left God's path to follow our own." –Isaiah 53:6

"For everyone has sinned, we all fall short of God's glorious standard." –Romans 3:23

"For the wages of sin is death, but the free gift of God is eternal life through Jesus Christ our Lord." –Romans 6:23

2. I believe that Jesus Christ is the way back to God.

"Jesus told him, I am the way, the truth, and the life. No one can come to the Father except through me." –John 14:6

"There is salvation in no one else! God has given no other name under heaven by which we must be saved." –Acts 4:12

"But God showed his great love for us by sending Christ to die for us while we were still sinners." –Romans 5:8

3. I repent of my sins and personally place my faith in Jesus Christ for eternal life.

"If you confess with your mouth that Jesus is Lord and believe in your heart that God raised him from the dead, you will be saved." –Romans 10:9

DEAR HEAVENLY FATHER,

I come to you today acknowledging that I am separated from you because of my sins. Thank you so much for loving me just as I am, and for sending your Son to die as a penalty for my sin. Today, I repent of my sins, and I personally place my faith in Christ. I confess that Jesus is Lord and I believe in my heart that you raised Him from the dead. Thank you that I can now have the assurance of eternal life! Please help me to walk with you, guided by the Holy Spirit, all the days of my life, and to trust you with everything I hold dear. In Jesus name, Amen.

Steps to Flourishing in Faith
—And the Journey Goes On —

Like a flower needing the essential nutrients, you too will need the nourishment of God's Word, prayer, and fellowship in order to flourish in your faith. The prayer you just spoke to God, sincerely prayed from the heart, is just the first step on your journey. These verses offer a glimpse into the process of growing into the image of Christ. May the path you walk be filled with jewels of wisdom, and whether you encounter sunshine or stormy weather, always remember the words Jesus left with His disciples: "I am with you always, even to the end of the age" (Matthew 28:20).

"And now, just as you accepted Christ Jesus as your Lord, you must continue to follow him. Let your roots grow down into him, and let your lives be built on him. Then your faith will grow strong in the truth you were taught, and you will overflow with thankfulness." –Colossians 2:6-7

"Remain in me, and I will remain in you. For a branch cannot produce fruit if it is severed from the vine, and you cannot be fruitful unless you remain in me." –John 15:4

"So faith comes by hearing, and hearing through the word of Christ." –Romans 10:17

"Like newborn babies, you must crave pure spiritual milk so that you will grow into a full experience of salvation." –1 Peter 2:2

"But if we confess our sins to him, he is faithful and just to forgive us our sins and to cleanse us from all wickedness." –1 John 1:9

"We will speak the truth in love, growing in every way more and more like Christ, who is the head of his body, the church. He makes the whole body fit together perfectly. As each part does its own special work, it helps the other parts grow, so that the whole body is healthy and growing and full of love." –Ephesians 4:15-16

For God loved the world so much that he gave his one and only Son, so that everyone who believes in him will not perish but have eternal life.
— John 3:16

Guidelines for Small Groups

INTRODUCTION

We are so delighted that you've chosen this coloring devotional to work through with your small group or Bible Study. It's unique in that the leader is more of a facilitator rather than a "teacher," and so most anyone versed in small group dynamics can host this group. We invite you to begin each session prayerfully and expectantly, and to anticipate a vibrant encounter with God as you observe the paintings, read the devotionals, journal, and color. May God guide you and fill you with all joy and peace as you encourage one another to flourish in your faith!

Time needed per session: Approximately 1 hour, for 15 weeks.

FACILITATOR'S AIM:

To set up a nurturing environment where women feel safe to connect and share.

To guide the group through each devotional and encourage authentic discussion.

PREPARATION NEEDED:

Create a warm inviting atmosphere in the room—choose soothing music (preferably without words), and plan some healthy light snacks.

Work through the coloring devotional topic prior to meeting.

Print an 8.5 x 11 colored copy of the painting and display it where all the ladies can see it.

Cover the time in prayer and trust God to use you for His glory.

SUGGESTED FLOW FOR EACH DEVOTIONAL:

Each coloring devotional has six pages and is divided into three sections—(1) The painting. (2) The Devotional. (3) The Journal and Coloring page. The following guidelines will help you to flow through each section.

- ❀ Greet the women and allow them time to connect and share some food and conversation. Soothing music can be playing in the background.

- ❀ Invite the ladies to get comfortable, and then open with prayer.

- ❀ Have them share their finished coloring pages from the previous week, then ask them to turn to the first page of the new topic.

- ❀ Begin by reading the "About The Painting" text.

- ❀ Then have them observe the painting. Ask, "What thoughts come to mind as you observe the colors, textures, movement and emotion in the painting?" Encourage them to share their thoughts.

- ❀ Ask them to turn to the devotional text and take turns reading out loud to the group.

- ❀ Then have them answer the study questions provided, while soothing music continues in the background.

- ❀ Invite them to turn to the coloring page that concludes each topic and share their answers while they color. Encourage discussion. Feel free to add your own questions if time permits. The atmosphere should be calm, relaxed, and friendly. (15 -20 minutes)

- ❀ As your time together winds down, remind them that although there is "No homework" (Yea!), to find some quiet time to finish the coloring page. Encourage them also to use the "Journal" page to revisit the verses, write a prayer, or just to share their thoughts on the topic.

- ❀ Thank the women for coming, and close in prayer. Let them know that you'll be excited to see their finished coloring pages the following week!

About the Authors

NATHALIE VILLENEUVE AND LEILA GRANDEMANGE love to create, one with her paint brush, the other with her pen. Their unique collaboration as painter and writer is aimed at helping women flourish in faith while experiencing God through the Creative Arts. Each of Nathalie's paintings and coloring pages is beautifully woven together with Leila's devotionals and is a testament to the magic that happens when women come together in friendship and faith. It is Nathalie's and Leila's sincere desire that this Coloring Devotional will awaken your creative core and encourage you to pursue the heart of God in every area of your life!

NATHALIE VILLENEUVE loves to weave self-expression, art, and faith into her message to help women cultivate their creativity. She defines herself as a free-spirited woman devoted to Christ and blessed with a loving family. Nathalie has a background in Fine Art and Graphic Design. She presently owns Pause and Paint and holds workshops where she helps women create art while raising their self-esteem. Nathalie's award-winning work speaks volumes and has been shown in various galleries, and recently as a greeting card line which can be found at Girlfriendsjourney.com. You can't help relating to her emotion on canvas art!

NathalieVilleneuve.com

PauseandPaint.com

LEILA GRANDEMANGE is a story teller at heart and loves sharing messages of hope! She's an author, award-winning writer, and the owner of Sunnyville Publishing. A former professional ballet dancer, Leila earned a B.A. in Christian Education with a minor in Bible. She loves all things creative and uses her background in education and the performing and visual arts to point people to Jesus Christ. Leila describes herself as devoted to God and family, an avid dog lover, and a work in progress in the hands of a loving God! She inspires faith through authentic communication and stories about God's amazing love. Connect with Leila at

LeilaGrandemange.com

SunnyvillePublishing.com

We invite you to continue this flourishing journey.
Please connect with us by visiting our websites at

NathalieVilleneuve.com
LeilaGrandemange.com

Love,
Nathalie & Leila

ORDER INFORMATION

Sunny Ville
PUBLISHING
www.sunnyvillepublishing.com

Please share a review on Amazon.com to invite others to experience a flourishing journey.

CPSIA information can be obtained at www.ICGtesting.com
Printed in the USA
BVIW12n0413111216
470391BV00011B/30